Table of Contents

Naomi,

Never leave the
Key to your happiness
in someone else's pocket.

Peace & blessings,
Divine Menelek
2/16

Messages for Joey

A Few Things I Need You to Know About:

Life

Friendship

Money

Love

Self

My Purpose

When I began writing this book, I was truly flooded with emotion. After having a conversation with my mom, I started wondering what would happen to my daughter, Jordyn (Joey), if I were no longer around to mother her. Having had her at what I affectionately term the "twilight of my life", the reality that she could possibly live a significant portion of her life without me to nurture and guide her did not go unrecognized. Although I am hoping to live for a very long time, the possibility of leaving her prematurely still breaks my heart tremendously.

It is for this reason that I began writing this book. My hope is that all of the lessons learned over the course of my lifetime will be imparted to her whether I'm here to personally share them with her or not. I want my daughter to have a practical guide for dealing with many of life's challenges without having to wonder, "What would my mom have said about this situation?" I want her to know where I stood on certain issues and what type of woman I hoped she would become. I realize that experience is one of our greatest teachers, however I hope that the words, opinions, and philosophies written in this book will save her some grief, and make her journey through this wonderment called life a little less confusing, complicated, or painful.

Although my messages are directed toward Joey, I'd like to offer inspiration to all of the other mothers, grandmothers, aunts, sisters, mentors and even dads who so desperately want to help a loved one navigate successfully toward womanhood, but sometimes simply can't find the right words to say. I pray that you'll deem the sentiments written here to be an appropriate expression of your own personal views and opinions, in regard to facing many of life's challenges. I also hope that you will take the opportunity to add your individual perspective, and any guidance which you'd like to convey to that special girl, in the space provided at the conclusion of each chapter.

As you read through these pages, you will find a compilation of advice based on lessons derived mostly from personal experience, as well as input received from various sources, most notably my mother, grandmothers, and a great grandmother whom I've never met but whose wisdom was passed down to me. Each adage is something to which I completely and wholeheartedly subscribe and strive to incorporate into my own life each and every day. Additionally, these messages are a true and honest reflection of what I believe it takes to be a successful woman, a kind and loving person, and a decent human being. I truly hope that these expressions will bring clarity, hope and peace to all who are in the process of navigating either themselves or a loved one through this wondrous blessing called life.

Joey, God has blessed me with the gift of writing, and now, I'd like to share my gift with you.

I love you Baby Girl.

Enjoy,
Mom

About Life:

Navigating the peaks, valleys and plateaus

Our upbringing, genetics and environment may have influenced our development but our direction in life is determined by our drive, dedication and desire to succeed. Nobody receives all 52 cards in the deck so play your best with the hand you've been dealt. Turn setbacks and excuses into challenges and motivation, and make the most of what you've got. There may be power in the victim status, but there is pride in overcoming the obstacles in your past and challenging others to do the same. Remember, the difference between a pit and a grave is how long you stay in it.

Get busy living or get busy dying. Don't be a pessimist who's always living under a cloud of doom and gloom while waiting for the other shoe to drop. Sometimes you're gonna get a bad deal because life isn't always fair. Neither joy nor misfortune are spread equally, and sometimes "bad things" do happen to "good people". Don't take it personally though, because that's just the way life is. Recognize that many people have accomplished a lot more with a lot less. So snap out of it, embrace the challenge in your situation, look toward the bright side, and keep it moving!

Everyone that looks like you is not your friend and everyone who doesn't is not your enemy. Sometimes the person whom you expect to have your back is the one who stabs you in it, and sometimes the person you expect to push you down is actually the one who lifts you up. Judge people by their deeds and character, not by their appearance, and practice viewing people as individuals, not as groups.

"No matter how badly your heart is broken, the world doesn't stop for your grief."* Although you may be falling apart inside, life around you will continue to move forward. Don't take this personally because, although others may empathize with your pain, for them life still goes on. Therefore, after taking time to properly grieve, you must prepare yourself to move forward. Remember, "No hour is ever eternity, but it has its right to weep."** Allow yourself that right, but recognize it as a chapter which has both a beginning and an ending.

*Author Unknown
** Zora Neale Hurston

Don't spend your life chasing others' dreams. Set your own goals and follow your own vision. There will always be people who feel as though they know what's best for you and who will try to determine your path. If their direction differs from yours, respectfully listen to their advice but always follow your own course. Who cares if you make mistakes along the way? A setback is never a failure if the experience taught you a good lesson. Be prepared to suffer the consequences of your well-intended decisions with maturity and grace, and know that in the end, whether successful or not, you were true to yourself and were the captain of your own ship.

Lock all of your doors and windows and never assume you are safe just because you are in a familiar area. Often predators are watching and waiting for you to let your guard down, so do not give them the opportunity to catch you "asleep". Be alert and aware of your surroundings at all times by limiting distractions and making yourself as unencumbered as possible. Don't put yourself in situations where people can take advantage of you because you left your possessions or your body in a vulnerable position. Don't make others responsible for your personal safety if you are placing yourself at risk by being intoxicated, careless or clueless. Ultimately, you are responsible for your own welfare, so don't get yourself into defenseless or irresponsible predicaments which can lead to victimization.

Sometimes you need to play in your good clothes, and let the wind mess up your hair. In other words, just live your life and enjoy each and every moment you have here. Cherish the small things and don't wait until there is a special occasion to pull out your new purse and shoes, because that day may never come. Instead, create your own holiday, and get all dressed up. Special occasions should not be determined by a calendar but by your desire to celebrate the joy, love and happiness within your own life. Each day is precious, so live it like it was your last.

Never leave home without enough plane, train or cab fare to get back. Although you might be going out with a group of great friends, or the love of your life, things happen and circumstances change. You might find yourself in a situation where you don't feel comfortable riding home with whomever you've arrived with, or may simply be ready to end the trip earlier than expected. Regardless of the situation, never allow yourself to be in a position where you are stranded, without resources, or are forced to rely on transportation from someone with whom you don't feel comfortable. If, when making plans, you realize that you will not have enough money to get home or elsewhere, then you should postpone your outing until you do.

Maturity is not about the number of candles on your birthday cake, but rather the trials, tribulations and experiences you've had and what knowledge you've acquired in the process. Simply being older does not necessarily make you wiser, more mature or more experienced than someone younger. Maturity comes from how you've faced, fought and conquered life's challenges, and what battle skills you've acquired along the way. So don't let the number of years a person has been on the planet be the determining factor as to whether they have the ability to teach you something.

Do not allow anyone to blame you for things that are not your fault. The fact that they consulted you or asked for your advice on something that did not turn out as they had planned or anticipated does not make their failure your fault. Do not allow yourself to be anyone's scapegoat. Once you take on that role it is very difficult to free yourself from its mental, psychological or emotional bondage. We are all born with free will and decision making ability. At the end of the day we are all responsible for the choices and decisions we make, so don't blame others for the outcome of yours and do not allow them to blame you for the outcome of theirs.

"**A**nything worth having is worth working for, and wanting something to happen is not the same as working hard toward making it happen."*
Be a go-getter and don't wait around for someone to show up at your door with an opportunity. Create your own opportunities by setting goals for yourself and working toward reaching them. So much time and energy is wasted waiting for someone to give you something that you can work hard to attain yourself. Setting your own goals also keeps others from establishing your limits. And since "luck" is the crossroads between opportunity and preparation, make sure you are adequately prepared when your opportunity arrives if you wanna get "lucky".

*Author Unknown

Learn the difference between wanting and needing, and be able to recognize when you truly have enough. Sometimes we spend so much of our lives in search of what we think will be our epitome of happiness or success when we often already possess that which we seek. It is impossible to have everything, so recognize the value and joy in your blessings and realize that it is actually through giving that we receive. Sure, there is power in owning, but there is satisfaction and beauty in creating, contributing and sharing with others.

L earn to view relationships as they really are and not as you would like them to be. Be able to recognize what you can control and differentiate it from what you cannot. Understand that you have absolutely no dominance over people, situations or outcomes, and that ultimately the only two things over which you do have control are your actions and your words. Countless hours can be wasted trying to influence the attitude, behavior, opinions or decisions of others. So if you determine that you've run into a brick wall in your futile attempt to change someone, simply turn around, regroup and reinvest your energy in to something over which you do have authority... <u>yourself</u>.

Trust but verify. Listen to what others have to say with an open mind but verify the truth in their statements prior to taking action. Follow up on information received before putting your name or reputation on the line. You would hate to run into battle with a dull sword, or to discover that the battle you are fighting is not even yours. Make sure to do your own research before involving yourself in someone else's cause or conflict.

Stop complaining and learn to be thankful for the simple things we take for granted. There are millions of people on the earth who dream about having clean running water, a sturdy roof over their head, a refrigerator full of food, adequate medical care, a warm bed and blankets, a vehicle, the opportunity to get an education, a safe home, a loving family and stability. Although life might seem rough at times, always be cognizant of how incredibly blessed you are to have at your fingertips what so many others long to experience.

Beauty comes from within, intelligence comes from experience and importance comes from respect. Don't assume that the spouse you're with, the house where you live, the car you drive, or the title you hold will make you any more beautiful, intelligent, or important. All of these attributes are indeed within your control but are not merely attached to you by your name, address, possessions or the company you keep. Additionally, don't confuse wealth with fortitude, power with integrity or affluence with honor. Just because someone has attained a particular status in life does not make them a good, honest or decent person. So don't get hung up on titles or visible attributes, but instead cultivate the qualities within yourself that are substantive, and surround yourself with others who do the same.

Talk less and listen more. God gave us two ears and one mouth for a reason. Spend time with the elderly and listen to what they have to say, they've been here a while and, believe it or not, they often know more than you do. Be patient with children and gentle with animals, neither are born with hatred or malice. Lead by example and recognize that others are watching every move you make and observing how you handle the pitfalls of life. Approach every person and situation as a learning experience, but understand that sometimes the opinions of others need to be taken with a grain of salt.

Better to have and not need than to need and not have. Pack an extra sweater, take a few extra dollars, get something to read in case you have downtime and grab a snack or a bottle of water before hitting the road. There's nothing worse than getting somewhere only to discover that you're unexpectedly cold, hungry or bored. It's far better to take a few seconds to grab something you might not need on the front end as opposed to being stuck in an uncomfortable situation because you didn't properly plan for an unforeseen situation down the road.

Recognize the substantial dangers of pride and ego. Additionally, understand that powerful, damaging feelings such as hostility, bitterness, jealousy, and rage must be acknowledged and rechanneled or they will interfere with your personal relationships, asphyxiate you, and create a toxic environment wherever you go. Never be too arrogant or stubborn to admit when you're wrong, and be willing to accept correction, direction and constructive criticism. Nobody knows everything and everyone has room to learn and grow, so don't allow your ego to get in the way of your moving forward mentally, physically, emotionally or professionally.

Don't burn your bridges; you never know when you'll need to cross them again. Whether you're leaving a job, a friendship or a romantic partner, try to do so with the least amount of drama possible. Even if you're parting on a sour note, make an effort to eliminate hostility and unkind exchanges. Instead, try to embrace the transition by focusing on a positive aspect of the relationship and the learning opportunity afforded by the experience. Maintaining composure and civility can go a long way, especially since you don't know who you'll need to vouch for you during a future reference or background check. Therefore, never let your final interaction with someone rewrite the entire history of your relationship, because your paths might very well cross again.

Never underestimate the power of your words and know that a smile from you can often bring happiness to someone else. You mean the world to someone, and you are special and unique in your own way. Sometimes people won't like you because they want to be just like you, but that's not your problem, it's theirs. So keep your head up, smile, be polite, and get on with your day.

Wasted time can never be replaced. Therefore, try to spend fewer moments being worried, troubled or angry, and more enjoying every precious second life has to offer. Recognize the beauty of the world around you and take more trips off the paved road. See things you've never seen before, taste foods you're never tasted, watch a movie with subtitles, explore other countries and cultures, and get to know your planet. Our time here is brief so try not to waste a single moment with useless emotions such as worry or stress. Live like every day is your last!

About Friendship:

Growing, showing and changing

Surround yourself with eagles not crabs. In other words, align yourself with those who want to fly, not with those who want to pull you down. Always associate with those who bring out the best in you and who support your strongest side, that way you'll never have to worry about getting involved with people or situations which cause you to make decisions that are not in your best interest. Always try to bring out the best in others and support their strongest side as well. Don't encourage someone you call a friend to do things which are not a positive representation of the person they claim to be. Remember, our friends and the company we keep are a reflection of ourselves.

Don't measure your worth or value by the number of friends you have. If you can get out of this life with one true, loyal friend then you have done well. Of course, it's nice to have a few more, but surrounding yourself with people just so you won't be alone does not guarantee happiness. The quantity of friends is not important, but the quality of those friendships is.

Steer clear of your friend's former romantic partners. There are far too many available companions in the world for you to cross that line. Although your friend may behave as though they are okay with it, it is a recipe for disaster. Since this is a very sticky area, and one for which the potential effect on your friendship is uncertain at best, do everyone a favor and steer clear of your friend's exes. Simply find someone else to date.

Don't be discouraged when friendships change. As you grow older people change, and sometimes you'll find yourself moving in a different direction than someone you consider a friend. This is a natural progression and, just as the seasons change, so do relationships with those we hold dear. Often these changes are for the best, as we strive to surround ourselves with those bringing positive energy into our lives. Furthermore, just because someone with whom you've spent every waking hour is no longer seated in your "front row" does not mean that that connection is lost forever. You don't have to see or speak to someone every day to appreciate what they've brought in to your life, or how they've shaped the person you've become.

Never let something replaceable come between you and a good friend. If you lend your friend money, do not expect to get it back. Therefore, if you do get it back, it will be a pleasant surprise, and if you don't, it won't strain the friendship. If you simply don't have the money to lend, then say so. It's better to be honest and tell your friend "No" than to feel resentful because you've gone without when you actually couldn't afford to do so. Money is replaceable and should never ever come between you and a good friend.

Stand up for your friend against others. When your friend is being attacked by the words of another, even without their knowledge, do not sit by and say nothing. Always take a stand or walk away. Never give the impression that saying unkind things or gossiping about your friend is okay with you. Just as you wouldn't want your friend to sit quietly while vicious things were being said about you, do not sit idly while others speak ill of them. It is never okay to be a coward.

The best way to have a good friend is to be one. Be the type of friend to others that you would want them to be to you. Don't gossip about your friend or betray their trust. If they tell you something in confidence, regardless of how juicy it may be, hold on to it with both hands. Just as you would not want your friend to tell others things you've shared with them, don't tell their secrets either. Even if your friend betrays your trust, that does not make it okay to betray theirs. Never define who you are by the actions of others. In other words, just because someone else turns out to be untrustworthy does not make it okay for you to become untrustworthy, too.

Learn not to take it personally when you are rejected by someone you'd like to be your friend. Just because someone does not want to be friends with you, play together, or hang out does not mean you are any less valuable or important. Just like some people prefer certain foods over others, people also have preferences about those with whom they choose to spend their time. Do not concern yourself with those who aren't interested in being around you. As long as you are being the best person you can be, you will always be cherished by those who truly love you and want to be in your company.

Try not to ever publicly disagree or argue with your friend. Just like family, a true friend is valuable and should never be chastised, ridiculed, devalued, cursed, attacked or berated maliciously in the presence of others. If you are angry or disappointed with your friend, speak with them about the issue privately and respectfully. The entire world does not need to know your personal business or the details of your conflict. If your friend tries to attack or argue with you publicly, do your best to maintain composure until you can move the discussion elsewhere. Any friend who insists on publicly attacking you may simply not be the person you believed them to be, and may not have the type of character of someone with whom you should continue to align yourself.

Never worry yourself, or place too much energy keeping count of the people who didn't come to your party. Sometimes people are busy, ill, or just don't want to come. Spending time and energy talking and thinking about those who did not show up is an insult to the ones who did. Celebrate those who want to celebrate with you, and be thankful for their presence, because they are the ones who made a point to be there. And the ones who didn't... well, they simply missed out on all the fun.

Take ownership of your actions and wrongdoings. Never be too proud or stubborn to apologize to your friend. At times, we all do or say things that we wish we could take back. Recognize when you have behaved in a way which angers your friend or causes them pain. Good friendships are hard to come by, and to throw one away simply because you cannot admit to being wrong is a sad statement about you. Furthermore, do not justify something you've done wrong to a friend by digging up something they did wrong to you "four scores and seven years ago". If you no longer want to be their friend then simply tell them so, but don't behave as though they've done something bad to you when you know in your heart that you are the one at fault.

The longer you let a rift between you and your friend continue the harder it will be to pick up the pieces and put things back together again. Never let anger or resentment fester for too long without discussing it with your friend. If, in the end, you decide to go your separate ways, then at least you are clear about where each of you stands. If you decide to remain friends, simply put the rift behind you and move on. Valuable time is wasted when you are at odds with someone you love, and time is one of the only things that we cannot get back once it is lost. Therefore, take pains to value not only your friends, but also every precious moment you have with them.

Sometimes you'll need to give your friend a break when they are too tired, sick or overwhelmed to go on a previously arranged outing. As you know, schedules or feelings can change and what seemed like a good idea when the plan was made may no longer seem either interesting or feasible. The same holds true for you. When you find yourself overloaded, or feel as though you have stretched yourself too thin, it's okay to respectfully decline an invitation or bow out of an event. True friends cut each other slack, as long as it isn't a constant occurrence, and they recognize that there are worse things in life than rescheduling, altering a plan or simply staying at home.

Do not distance yourself from your friend when they are hurting. Often people don't know what to do or say when someone they consider a good friend experiences loss, grief or pain. There is never any way to relieve the pain of another, but remaining side by side with your friend and allowing them the opportunity to talk, cry, scream or simply sit quietly will let them know that you are there for them and they are loved. Even though your friend may try to push you away, realize that they are hurting and need you now more than ever. Although their pain may last for a very long time, maybe even forever, take comfort in knowing that you stood beside them in their time of need and did everything you could to support them.

N ever take your friends for granted. Take time to let them know how much you appreciate them. Remember them on holidays, attend their special events, and embrace the things that are important to them. Celebrate their successes and offer comfort in their moments of defeat. Pray for them. Always encourage them to do their best, even when their best turns out to be better than yours. Remember, friendships are like flowers. If you don't nurture them, they will die.

"No matter how good a friend is, recognize that they are going to hurt you every once in awhile and that you must forgive them for that."* Just as it is important to own up to mistakes and hurtful things you've done or said to a friend, it is also important to allow them the same grace. There will be times you'll feel slighted by your friend, but allow them the opportunity to make things right and offer them the gift of forgiveness. We are all human and we all make mistakes. Therefore, you cannot hold your friend to a higher level of perfection than you hold yourself. Remember, "Let he without sin cast the first stone."**

*Author Unknown
**John 8:7

Never underestimate the power of your words or actions. When speaking with your friend, always try to be free with praise and gentle with criticism. Every opinion does not need to be verbalized and choose your words carefully if your words might cause pain. With one small gesture or expression you can change the direction of a person's life forever, for better or for worse. We are all put in each other's lives to have an impact in some way, so always try to build up and support your friend whenever possible. Remember, "Friends are angels who lift us to our feet when our wings have trouble remembering how to fly."*

*Author Unknown

Learn to distinguish between true friends and "ride-alongs". As time goes on, you should be able to identify which of your friends are willing to go into battle with you, and which are just hanging on for the ride. I once heard it said that "a friend will help you move, but a true friend will help you move a body." Know which type you're dealing with and conduct your relationships accordingly. Although it's okay to keep light-weight friends in your life, be aware of where they fall on your list of priorities and, as my father used to say, "Keep em' in front of you."

Always be your own person and not simply a follower or clone of your friend. Have your own thoughts, opinions and ideas, and stand your ground on what you think is right. Don't get caught up in what's popular when what's popular is wrong. Do not let anyone, not even your friend, encourage you to turn against your moral, ethical or personal values. If you believe your friend is headed in the wrong direction, or is making a decision which you feel in your heart is a mistake, don't just go along with the program for the sake of friendship. Tell them how you feel. If they make the wrong choice anyway, try your best to comfort them when they fall. In essence, if your friend were to jump off a cliff, don't jump with them, just wait at the bottom and try to help them when they land.

A lways make time to spend with your closest girlfriends. You must realize that life, work, romantic relationships, or other commitments should never inhibit your ability to spend occasional time with those you hold dear. Taking time out to laugh, share and reconnect with "the girls", is an essential part of mental and spiritual well being. I have friends who I don't see or speak with very often, but when we finally do get together, it's as if we've never left each other's side. That's why it's so important to "check in" with those special people in your life, because they know you better than anyone, and you know them just as well. Although everyone else may hear what you say, girlfriends listen to what you <u>don't</u> say. So, regardless of how busy you are, carve out time to kick back and take guiltless pleasure in time well spent with friends.

About Money:

Earning, managing and career building

Money does not buy happiness. You can be a miserable millionaire or a jubilant homeless person. Yes, it's nice to live without financial problems or stress but money can also cause relationships to crumble and friendships to end. Never put the pursuit of money before the people who matter most, and don't assume that having money will automatically make you happy.

Save! Save! Save! You have no idea what hardship awaits. Whether it's getting your car repaired, an unexpected trip out of town or a new outfit for a last-minute event, you never want to be financially unprepared. Therefore, make sure you always have as much as possible set aside and available in case of an emergency.

Avoid using credit to purchase things for which you should use cash. Anything with a short-use duration such as food, entertainment or other temporary expenses should not be financed with a credit card, unless you intend to pay the bill in full at the end of the month. If you carry the balance over for months from groceries purchased on a credit card, you are in essence continuing to pay for something that is long gone. Therefore, either use cash or pay the credit balance in full when charging temporary items.

Never discuss your finances with others, and don't share details about how much money you've won, earned, saved or borrowed. Sometimes people will try to use this information to take advantage of you, or they might attempt to talk you into contributing to their investment scheme. If you choose to invest, do so wisely and after thorough investigation, professional consultation and exhaustive research. Don't ever let someone who's broke talk you into investing in something they're peddling. "A fool and his money will soon be parted..."

Always leave some wiggle room in your budget. Don't make a purchase for which the payments hardly leave you with enough leeway to live comfortably from day to day. It doesn't make sense to buy a brand new car when you can barely keep food in the refrigerator. Recognize what your means are and live within them. Be prepared to make sacrifices when things get tight, such as making your lunch instead of eating out, dropping some of your luxury expenses, and throwing your old sneakers in the wash instead of buying new ones. Sometimes you'll need to be thrifty in order to live comfortably.

*A*lways keep a small "emergency stash" for yourself, which is not comingled with the household funds. You might want to treat yourself to something special, or offer assistance to your children, and may have neither the time nor desire to obtain authorization from all interested parties. Maintaining your own "reserve fund" allows you the flexibility for those spur-of-the-moment expenses. So, in other words, make sure you always have your own money so that you can do with it what you please, when you please.

Don't ever allow yourself to be controlled or dictated by money. You have the strength, the intelligence and the resources to make your own way in this world. Don't be subjected to someone holding your purse strings or dangling money over your head. It's better to be a hard-working person with dignity than a puppet at someone else's mercy. God bless the child who has her own.

Spend your time building up your own kingdom instead of worrying about the assets of others. Choose an education and career path which will allow you to achieve your own comfortable standard of living. Don't waste time competing with others when you can spend that energy investing in yourself and your future.

ake sure you are financially stable and professionally secure before entertaining the prospect of marriage and kids. It's hard enough trying to make ends meet by yourself, but once you add a spouse and kids to the mix the stress level can become unbearable. Therefore, make sure you are adequately educated, properly insured and gainfully employed prior to beginning the conversation of marriage and kids. Additionally, make sure your potential mate is equally stable and secure.

Don't count other people's money. Although someone else might seem to have it all together financially, that doesn't mean they do. You never know what type of hardships people are dealing with, so just because a person or family seems wealthy that doesn't mean they're not struggling. And just because someone lives a modest lifestyle, that doesn't mean they're not wealthy. It's always best to practice minding your own financial business rather than concerning yourself with others' economic affairs.

Remember that your job application is the first impression most employers will have of you, and often the most significant. Therefore, make sure you complete each application as thoroughly and accurately as possible. Don't answer questions with brief answers or partial sentences but rather make yourself stand out by highlighting your unique abilities via responses that personally address each question. Also, avoid using words like "feel", "think" or "believe" when characterizing your attributes on application questions. These are passive words and should typically be replaced with more confident terms such as "am certain", "know" and "undoubtedly". Your potential employer needs to know that you are confident in your ability to do the job, rather than simply "hoping" you can get it done.

You won't be young and healthy forever, so as soon as you are able, transition yourself from a job to a career with a retirement plan, healthcare and benefits. I know this seems an eternity away, but the sooner you begin planning for your financial future, the less running around you'll find yourself doing down the road. Many people work their entire lives without ever obtaining a financial safety net for their later years. They end up having to work until they die or until they no longer have any real quality of life left. Don't let that happen to you. Start planning for your golden years as early as possible.

Be on time, which actually means be a few minutes early. It's not good to be known as the person who is always late for everything because it makes others view you as being less dependable. Arriving early for work, school or an appointment allows you the opportunity to gather your thoughts and materials, or to have a bit of time left over to socialize or relax. Having to rush around because you are running late leads to disorganization, forgetfulness and being generally frazzled. So try to plan your schedule in such a way that will allow time to catch your breath and present yourself in a calm, relaxed and confident manner.

Always go to your job interview prepared to ask two questions of the interviewer, even if you already know the answers. Questions such as, "Is there room for advancement here?" or "What type of personality characteristics best fit into your organizational structure?" are direct inquiries and show the potential employer that you are ready to adapt yet highly motivated to succeed. If you don't ask any questions at the conclusion of an interview it gives the interviewer the impression that you already know everything... and nobody wants to hire a know-it-all. Therefore, express genuine interest in the position by formulating additional questions to present at the conclusion of the interview.

Your credit rating is extremely important and will have a definite impact on your quality of life. Failure to pay bills on time, maxing out your credit cards, frivolous spending and being irresponsible with financial commitments is the fastest way to ruin your credit score. This will affect your ability to purchase a car, rent an apartment, secure a loan, buy a house and, yes, even to get a job. Pay what you owe and don't bite off more than you can chew. Recognize financial decisions which can negatively impact your credit and steer clear of those traps. It takes a few poor choices to ruin your credit and a lifetime of conscientious behavior to repair it.

Practice being a team player. Whether you're working on a group project or in a supervisory position, you will be far more successful and effective if you evaluate the strengths and weaknesses of those working alongside you and use your personal talents to help make the team stronger. Since a chain is only as strong as its weakest link, do your part in supporting team members who might be struggling to keep up. Additionally, when you find yourself working with others in a group capacity, recognize that it's not all about you and be cognizant of the fact that, in these settings, success only comes as a result of effective collaboration.

Always be prepared to ask a question during the Q&A portion of a job fair or recruiting information forum. Raising your hand and asking the presenter(s) a thoughtful, intelligent, relevant question shows that you are assertive, interested, bright, articulate and unafraid to stand out in a crowd. It is, in essence, your first interview opportunity because you never know who is in the room and potentially impressed by your confidence or inquisitiveness. Sitting quietly in a room full of potential candidates and electing to say nothing is the equivalent of not having been there at all. What's the point of going to the event if you do nothing to separate yourself from the crowd? So get names, shake hands, ask questions and do whatever you can to make your professional presence known.

If you borrow money from someone, pay them back as soon as you possibly can. It is both inconsiderate and rude to spend money on frivolous things while you are in debt on a personal loan. Believe me, the person you borrowed from is noticing your new shoes, new purse or constant vacations and is wondering when and if you are planning to return their money. Save them from having to inquire as to when you plan to repay the loan, and simply pay them back. This type of thing most definitely ruins relationships.

Constantly increase your knowledge base by learning a new language, enrolling in a challenging course, doing volunteer work, applying for an internship, mastering a new skill, getting involved in a club or organization, advocating for change, traveling outside of your comfort zone, attending others' religious and cultural events or taking on a seemingly impossible task. You will need to pull from these experiences throughout your lifetime, as they will assist you in gaining credibility in both your professional and personal life. People tend to listen to what you say when they realize you've been places and seen things that they haven't. It establishes your authority and gains their respect.

Whenever possible, donate to charity and give to the poor. If you have been blessed with means and stability, share those blessings with others who are less fortunate. Don't turn your nose up at those who have fallen on hard times and be cognizant of the fact that, "But for the grace of God, go I."* You might one day be standing in their shoes needing food, shelter or a compassionate smile. Be gracious and humble ALWAYS.

* John Bradford

About Love:

Finding, keeping and letting go

"He who findeth a wife findeth a good thing",* not she who clunks him over the head and drags him back to her cave. Don't be too aggressive or appear desperate when it comes to dating. A man will know you're interested simply by the way you smile and say "Hello". Regardless of what agenda modern society attempts to push, most men like to pursue and give chase. Allow them that opportunity. In the meantime, focus on being a non-needy, mentally, emotionally, morally grounded and stable person, who is likely to attract the same.

* Proverbs 18:22

Although love is wonderful, it should never be the sole determining factor in choosing a life partner. It is important to evaluate a person's character, mental stability, temperament, maturity, earning potential, availability, sincerity, willingness and capacity to commit before making a decision based solely on love. Yes, love is nice, but when it comes to choosing your mate for life and the father of your children, love is only one of MANY things to be considered.

Just because you're angry with the person you love, does not mean you have the right to be cruel or disrespectful. Choose your words and actions carefully, even when angry, and make them soft enough to eat, just in case you have to do so at a later time. You most likely won't be mad forever so avoid doing and saying things that you'll regret. Remember, three things which you can never get back are time once it has passed, words once they've been spoken, and the stone once it has been thrown.

Leave the baggage from a past relationship in the past and be open to love and companionship prior to entering a new commitment. If you are not mentally or emotionally stable enough for a new partner then don't bother dragging anyone else into your life until such time that you are able to share your healthiest self. Jumping from one relationship to another without first taking time to regroup and reflect upon what happened is neither smart nor healthy. Therefore, take time to make sure you are mentally and emotionally ready to date again. Damaged goods are not attractive.

Marry someone who loves you more than you love them and you'll spend a lot less time crying. Being in an unequal relationship where you are making all of the emotional sacrifices or putting in the majority of the work to keep things afloat is not only tiresome, but has a tendency to breed resentment down the road. Being overly invested in someone who is not as invested in you is a bad move. Therefore, try to find a partner who simply adores you, and treats you as though you are the queen of his world, thus decreasing the likelihood of you being disrespected, unappreciated, or abandoned in years to come. Remember to never make someone your priority when you are only one of their options.

Know that just because someone does not love you the way that you'd like to be loved, does not mean they do not love you in the best way that they can. Relationships will not always be at the level you'd like for them to be but that does not mean the love of your life is not giving their all. Be patient and recognize when someone is giving 100% of themselves, even if that is only 50% of what you want. It is better to end a relationship with someone who is unable to live up to your romantic expectations rather than stay with them and continue to try to force them into being someone they're not.

Look for a potential life partner who can teach you something new. Don't get stuck in the role of the person who is always the teacher, motivator, and introducer of new life experiences. Try to find a mate who has been places you have not, learned things you did not know, or can teach you something new. It becomes very boring when you are the only one in the relationship who does or has ever done anything new, interesting or exciting. In other words, try to choose a relationship where you won't be the only one doing the teaching, motivating and inspiring, and if you find that you are, then encourage your partner to expand their knowledge or experience base. It makes for boring conversation when you are the sole provider of new information.

Make sure a potential spouse has had an active role model and significant training on how to treat a woman with class, dignity and respect. He should not expect you to change your own tire on the side of the road while he sits in the passenger seat, go to the store after dark for something he could run out and purchase for you, or wait alone on a dark curb for him to drive the car around. Your mate needs to understand, without a doubt, that his role in the family is that of protector, provider and base. He should not expect to pass his responsibilities off on you, nor should you be willing to accept such. Sure, there are situations and circumstances where responsibilities in the household are redistributed, but roles are not interchangeable and you should never allow anyone to transfer theirs to you. Remember, a "real woman" may be able to do it all, but a "real man" won't stand by and watch her while she does.

When you argue or disagree with your mate it does not mean you don't love each other, and when you don't argue and disagree it does not mean that you do. Sometimes happy couples argue and sometimes miserable couples appear to be perfect. Therefore, don't look at an argument or rough patch in your relationship as a sign of impending doom. Since every couple experiences peaks and valleys, relationship altering decisions should rarely be made following one incident or rough period.

Good credit is an essential characteristic in choosing a mate. A potential spouse who has no control over their own finances and spending habits will likely be unable to manage the household funds as well. Any prospective partner who tells you that having good credit is not important probably has bad credit, and should be evaluated as a possible relationship risk.

Nobody wants to deal with a person who constantly has a bad attitude, an unfriendly disposition or a sharp tongue. When someone greets or compliments you, rather than assuming they are flirting or attempting to harass, just be polite, cordial and respond appropriately. There is no need to be arrogant in your interactions with others, or to walk around with a chip on your shoulder. Exchanging pleasantries is not a marriage proposal and a smile does not have to be an invitation for intimacy. Additionally, don't pride yourself on being "difficult to handle" in relationships, since only animals and inanimate objects should be "handled". Just relax and practice being courteous and gracious when dealing with others, just as you would like for them to be when dealing with you.

Look for a mate who does not have to be the center of attention or whose sole motivation is not constant adoration and praise from others. A person who has an incessant need for attention will constantly seek out situations and relationships where they can be a hero and placed on a pedestal. Unfortunately, your pedestal may not be the only one on which they find themselves in their never-ending search for ego gratification. Therefore, look for a partner who is self-motivated and is a "go getter", driven by things other than a constant need to be needed.

Be leery of romantic partners who've left a trail of unfinished projects. If he was five credits away from attaining his BA, five dollars short from starting his own business, or five pages away from finishing his novel then he likely has a very short attention span and is unlikely to follow through and complete much of anything... perhaps even your relationship.

Be careful when receiving marital advice from others, especially those with no relevant experience. Often people who are miserable or have had broken marriages will try to impose upon you the baggage from their own failed relationships. They will do their best to attempt to talk you out of your marriage or lure you away from your partner. Recognize that sometimes people have an agenda and aren't truly interested in what's best for you. Be leery of someone who constantly points out the negative traits in your partner, or offers unsolicited advice about your marriage. In fact, don't get into the habit of incorporating others into the fabric of your relationship at all, whether they're married or not, regardless of how well meaning they may appear to be.

Yes, contrary to popular belief it DOES matter what type of family your mate comes from and on which side of the tracks he grew up. People are products of their environment and although it does not always show initially, the ideals and values of individuals are rooted in their childhood experiences and may sometimes display themselves unfavorably. For example, is he from a family ripe with broken marriages or deadbeat dads? Is there a history of addiction or mental-health issues in his past? Was he abandoned or abused by either or both parents? Is he from an elitist family filled with racist, sexist or social intolerance? Try as you might, you cannot fix a broken or closed-minded person and you will become resentful in the process of attempting to do so. Save yourself some grief and look for someone who is mentally and emotionally healthy, and perhaps who comes from the same religious and social perspective as yourself. The objective here is to not have to work too hard in any relationship, because marriage should not be constantly competitive or exhausting. I'm not saying marriage is easy, but it should not feel like a full-time job either.

A suitable relationship partner is someone with the maturity of an adult, not the temperament of a child. You don't need a pouter, a hitter, a punisher, or a partner who is totally unable to make a single decision for himself. You should not be placed into the role of being your mates mother, and if you find the relationship heading in this direction then run for your life. Once the real children come along your growing resentment towards your spouse may turn to bitterness, which will not be healthy for any of the parties involved.

Never try to force a round peg into a square hole. Sometimes, especially in relationships, you want something so badly that you will try to reconstruct reality in order to make it happen. Too often you won't achieve the desired result, which leads to the old adage of "may you get what you want and may it be what you meant." No matter how much you may want someone to be available, or to love you the way that you'd like, you cannot force the issue. Therefore, try to recognize when someone is unavailable, or is simply not a good relationship fit, and move on.

When someone you're dating displays their true character, believe them. Usually people will put their best foot forward when they are first getting to know you and trying to make a good impression. If he acts like a jerk during the courting process, chances are... he's a jerk. Never ignore obvious character flaws and signs of blatant incompatibility. If you attempt to gloss over these things and try to convince yourself that observations are mirages and intuition is paranoia, then it won't be long before you realize you've made a big mistake, wasted a lot of time, and don't have anyone else to blame but yourself.

Never sacrifice who you are in order to keep peace in a relationship. Never turn away from your family, your friends, your religion or anything else that is significant or important to you as an individual. When you start giving up more and more of yourself, your dreams, or the essence of who you are, you become a shell of the person you once were. This is a terrible place to find yourself because one day you will look in the mirror only to discover that you are face-to-face with a total stranger.

Do not get involved in a relationship with anyone who is a mental or emotional drain, or a vexation to your spirit. Try to stay away from those who only want to take from you and sap your energy, while giving little in return. Try to involve yourself with someone who provides a positive addition to your life, someone who makes you laugh, who provides good conversation, who stimulates you mentally, and who encourages you to let your hair down and have a good time. Remember, you'll have your own problems and, unless it is your paid profession, you do not have time to constantly help your partner work through his. Therefore, be prepared to extract yourself from relationships with those who add undue stress and who do not provide a positive addition to your life.

It is just as easy to fall in love with a rich person as it is to fall in love with a poor person. Yes, there are wonderful dating options on all rungs of the financial ladder, but since money is the root of many relationship problems, eliminating the stress which results from financial difficulties can carry you a very long way. A romantic partner who has the means, the drive, the potential and the work ethic to take care of the family and pay the bills is able to help reduce the anxiety and pressure on the relationship that comes from having a lack of funds. No one says you have to live in a mansion, but quality of life is important and lack of financial resources to provide for the family definitely diminishes one's quality of life. So once again, it's just as easy to fall in love with a rich person as it is to fall in love with a poor person, and a heck of a lot less stressful.

A closed mouth does not get fed. You have to speak up for what you want in your life. In a relationship, you need to spell out exactly what you need to be happy and exactly what you want for your man to do for you. Men are not mind readers and don't do well with evaluating subtle clues. You cannot expect your man to simply know what you want unless you ask, and you cannot blame him for not being psychic. Therefore, don't give hints. Say what you mean and mean what you say, which can be accomplished in a way that is not consistently negative, rude, aggressive, argumentative or confrontational. Remember, you can catch more flies with honey than vinegar and, in the end, your message will be much better received.

It's always good to marry your best friend and confidant. Regardless of how hot and steamy a relationship is at first, the passion might not always remain at the same level and there had better be something else to take up the slack. Having something in common other than children, lust and physical attraction is critical to the success of your marriage. Mutual respect, trust, and the ability to work as a team must also be key elements in your relationship. Even the best marriages suffer times of shock, disappointment, failure, and trouble. However, a strong foundation keeps the union safe and sound. So work to develop common interests in order to ensure that you will always have several shared connections with one another. Additionally, build a solid wall around your relationship to effectively keep out meddlers, busy bodies and negative outside influences.

About Self:

Cultivating a healthy mind, body and spirit

The content of your character is measured by your actions. What you do determines who you are and who you are will therefore determine what you do. Evil, spiteful and negative people do evil, spiteful and negative things. Loving, caring, honest and sincere people behave in ways that are loving, caring, honest and sincere. It does not matter who you SAY you are, it only matters who you SHOW you are.

Don't take rejection personally. If someone knocked on my door and offered me a million-dollar ruby I would pass because I have no use for a million-dollar ruby. That does not mean the ruby is any less valuable because I chose to pass, I just made a different choice. Just because someone passes on you as a date, partner or friend does not diminish your value; it only means they made a different choice. Brush it off and don't take it personally.

Sometimes saying nothing speaks volumes. There is power in silence, and occasionally, rather than speaking up and saying what's on your mind, it is far more effective to simply remain silent. This is not the same as the old adage of "If you don't have anything nice to say, say nothing." What I'm referring to is that every now and then it's better to just keep quiet and allow the words of another to deflect off of you without giving a response. At times remaining quiet keeps you from saying things you'll later regret. At other times being silent denies the person with whom you are in conflict the reaction that they are desperately trying to elicit. So recognize that it is not always time to speak, and that sometimes, through your silence, you've said more than your words ever could.

Being alone is not the equivalent of being lonely. Learn to be at peace with yourself and enjoy your own company. Don't be the type of person who always needs to have someone else around in order to feel happy or secure. Some of the best moments in life are spent alone and in quiet, peaceful reflection. When you are content with yourself and comfortable with silence, you are in a better place to relax, meditate and become more acquainted with that little voice inside of you which is all too often ignored.

"Every shut eye ain't sleep and every goodbye ain't gone."* Watch what you say and do when in the company of someone who looks to be asleep or purports to have left the room. You never really know who is listening to what you say, especially when the person appears to be unaware of, or oblivious to, the conversation. Therefore, watch what you say around others, even when you think they're not listening, or out of hearing range. Overheard statements and observed actions have been known to come back to bite.

* Carrie Swan

Being forgiven by others is important, just as it is equally important to forgive yourself. We all make mistakes, sin and come short of the glory of God. Don't continue to berate yourself for transgressions you have taken ownership of, apologized for and vowed to correct. Additionally, don't allow others to revisit atoned for mistakes or behaviors for which you are less than proud. Once you have done your best to repair a situation or relationship, move on.

Profanity is for those who have run out of, or are unfamiliar with, the proper words to use in a given instance. Profane diatribes scream of ignorance and ones inability to express themselves as a sane, rational, intelligent human being. Therefore, make sure you speak to others in a way that is a positive reflection of the intelligence and maturity you wish to project, and reject the negative energy of those who choose to predominately address you and others through the use of profanity, vulgarity and disrespectful terms.

"Don't stir in old poop, it starts to stink."* Sometimes things are simply better left alone. Let sleeping dogs lie and don't keep revisiting old issues, gripes or grief if the visit will serve no productive purpose. Once you have effectively worked through an issue with a friend, coworker or romantic partner, why keep bringing it up? Often rehashing the same resolved dispute over and over does nothing but make your current situation worse, as it causes the "poop" to start stinking again. So leave it alone and turn the page.

* Carrie Swan

Either you control your attitude or it controls you. How you perceive or react to a situation is half the battle. If you decide to see the glass as half empty, it will be so. However, if you decide to see the glass half full, then you'll find plenty of room left to top it off. You can typically control your day by the mental tape you play in your mind. The energy you buy in to determines the aura you give off. So put on a coat of power, confidence, and peace each morning to help you navigate through the day's challenges.

Stand up for yourself. Just because someone has a different opinion or perspective does not make them right or wrong, just different. There's no need to take things personally. Simply evaluate their position, accept or reject their viewpoint and move on. Conversely, don't allow yourself to be silenced because someone else does not agree with your point of view. Why should your ideas or opinions be any less valuable than theirs? Never allow yourself to be bullied into taking someone else's position on anything. Remember: If you lie down like a doormat then expect for people to step on you... and likely wipe their feet.

It is always okay to admit you've made a mistake and to try to correct it. I don't care if it's a bet, a dare or the eve of your wedding, it is usually not too late to back out of a bad decision. Never go through with something you know in your heart is wrong in order to appease others or to save face. No matter what the predicament, make sure you make the decision that best suits you and is in line with your morals, your values, your beliefs, and your mental and emotional wellbeing.

You can do something in an instant that will give you heartache for a lifetime. Make sure your decisions are thoughtfully considered and that you are prepared for any foreseeable consequences. So many mistakes and life-altering decisions are made in moments of haste, anger or idiocy. Remember, every action has a reaction, so always try your best to evaluate what that reaction will be and strive to live your life with no regrets. Of course no one can foresee the future, but relying upon the experience and wisdom of those you trust and respect might help you to avoid some of life's inevitable pitfalls. Yes, 1 know knowledge often comes from making mistakes, but sometimes it's okay to learn from the mistakes of others instead of having to make them all yourself.

Sometimes you're gonna have to smile even when you don't feel like it. Attitude determines behavior just as much as behavior determines attitude. If you bring bad energy or a negative disposition into a room, it will likely remain there and become contagious. Of course you'll have days when you simply don't feel like smiling or being upbeat, but recognize that the harder the rain falls the prettier the rainbow, and that this too shall pass. Being grumpy, moody and irritable can become habit forming so put some pep in your step, turn that frown upside down, and don't ever get comfortable being a grouch.

Take care of your mental and emotional health. We all have times when we feel overwhelmed and may need to seek professional assistance in dealing with a particularly disturbing event or situation. Do not ignore the damage that stress can do to your body, and recognize that it can actually kill you. Continuing to walk around like everything is okay while you are crumbling inside is neither wise nor necessary. So please, don't ever hesitate or be too proud or ashamed to seek whatever physical, mental or emotional help is needed to ensure that you are the healthiest and most productive person you can be.

Don't live in the past. We all have special moments and experiences that we wish could last forever, but they simply can't. Enjoy them while they're here, and then gracefully let them go. Embrace the joy found in sharing old memories with loved ones, or giggling to yourself about times past. Recognize that, although these events and relationships molded you into who you are, they must now share space with new experiences that will write the chapter on who you will become. So "don't cry because it's over...smile because it happened."*

* Dr. Seuss

Don't get used to bending over backwards or changing lanes simply because your opinion or the assertion of your needs makes someone feel uncomfortable. You have just as much right to be seated in the front row as anyone else, so don't get into the habit of jumping into the "back seat" just to placate others. Once you've established yourself as someone who constantly bends and yields to the whims of those around you, people will begin expecting you to crouch down just so that they can get a better view. You deserve to be treated with kindness and respect, and understand that it is never okay to set yourself on fire in order to keep others warm.

Since you've only been given one body, do your very best to take care of it. Get enough rest, drink more water, eat a well-balanced diet and try to squeeze in a little exercise here and there. Take time to feed your soul, renew your spirit and relax your mind by laughing, dancing, playing, praying and sitting on the beach. Never ignore physical ailments and schedule regular check-ups, even when you're feeling fine, because what aches you today might actually kill you tomorrow. It's always okay to exhibit modesty and decorum, and be aware that if you maintain respect for your body and demand the same from others, you will undoubtedly cultivate a much greater sense of value and self-worth.

Recognize when it's time to walk away. Whether from a relationship, a job, a friendship, a fight or any other sort of toxic situation, at times it's best to simply turnaround and leave. Sometimes you'll come to the realization that your current environment is harmful, unhealthy or detrimental to your overall wellbeing. Rather than hanging around until things further deteriorate, give yourself permission to throw in the towel. Don't berate yourself or allow others to condemn you for doing so either, since it's likely advantageous for them to keep you around. Therefore, when you determine it to be unsafe, unhealthy or unwise to remain in your current situation, then by all means, gracefully and respectfully WALK AWAY.

Stand for something. Recognize that there are many things in this world that need fixing and challenge yourself to help make something better. Your voice is powerful so use it for more than just singing in the shower. Speak up against hatred and injustice, be an advocate for change, think outside of your own bubble and do your best to find a way to positively impact the world around you. As you learned in Girl Scouts, "Always leave a place better than you found it." So find something you're passionate about, roll up your sleeves and get busy making a difference!

Hold yourself accountable and don't make anyone else responsible for your success or failure. Take control of your path in life, and if you get bumped off along the way, find a new path. If it is meant for you, it will be yours, and if it is not, then it won't. Make a vow never to betray yourself, lose faith, or abandon hope in what you believe you can achieve. Never settle for less than you deserve, and don't ever give up trying... remember, you can keep going long after you think you can't. Brush off doubt and cynicism, keep yourself in the game, and make a commitment to approach each day with open eyes, an open heart, an open mind and a willing spirit to fully embrace every amazing opportunity life has to offer.

Final Thoughts

So there it is Joey, almost everything I think you'll need to know in order to get off on the right foot. You are such a blessing to me and I have truly loved writing this book for you. I want you to recognize your unique gift as a peacemaker who has the ability to bring people together, so keep letting your little light shine. Remember that you are perfectly and wonderfully made, therefore don't consume yourself with doubt or anxiety about who you are or what you were created to be.

I pray that you will always stand strong on your faith and on your principles, and that you will not stray from your core values or deviate from your moral compass. But if you should stumble off course, and perhaps even fall as we all do sometimes, simply pick yourself up, dust yourself off, and get back in the ring. Remember that beauty and strength may fade but character never does, so always try your hardest, give it your best and strive to make each and every day count. But most importantly, always remember that neither time nor space nor distance will separate me from you, because I am with you always, and I will love you forever and ever and ever...

Made in the USA
Middletown, DE
26 June 2016